HEART OF THE
POET

GERBIN MICHE

Inks and Bindings
888-290-5218
www.inksandbindings.com
orders@inksandbindings.com

CONTENTS

PRETTY

Oh, pretty woman! Your lips
has the color of red wine
and the sweetness of life, your
beauty has the enchantment of heaven,
when I think of you, eternity
is a step away.

Oh, pretty! God made you
as a real treasure, a real woman,
goddess of goddesses, you, you are
a classic verse of poet, muse
of angels, you are the
poetry of King David.

Your beauty has
the freshness of a romantic morning,
a pleasant scent, the dark yellow
of sunflowers.

Words aren't enough to say who you are.

You're the garden where seeds bloom; the
water when there is no rain, the light
where there is no sun, lightning in
darkness; the stars
that glow brightly, the rainbow
over the rivers.

CARNATION

I found a flower in my life; her name
is: I don't know yet, but
I'm sure she's like
white cloud, her beauty
has a touch of magic, her
rainy voice enchanted my soul,
every time I see her, my heart
beats a lot.

I found a flower
in my life, she is a real treasure,
the green pearl that
I was looking for.

I'm so blessed; from now on, she is
the sun in my blue sky, the soil
where the seeds of my feelings bloom.
Even though she is not with me yet, I will love
her the way I love her today.

JOURNEY

I took a long walk (half of my life)
looking for you, and now
here we are; I will hold
your hand to finish
the journey together.

ECLIPSE

Oh, darling! Today we love
each other, like two planets,
distant, far away,
but under the
same sky, the same orbit.
The day will come, we will
be one, our love will
be seen by the whole world
as a total eclipse.

HEART OF A POET

I would to have
a heart of a poet to tell you
beautiful things, I would want
to have a heart of a guitar to
sing to you everything that
I think, but I don't have a
heart of a guitar, and I have
no spirit of a poet.
Lady, with these humble
words, let me tell you that you are
an enchanted orchid, your
beauty is like gold; always shining,
your eyes, two beautiful stars that
light up the night,
your voice is like the rain
in a magic garden.
Oh, pretty woman! Your tenderness
perfumes my mind and
covers me with inspiration,
every time I see you, I feel
the universe is near me.

Woman, you are my inspiration,
my music, you are my poetry,
you are my whole life.

HOLD

Hold me in your hands;
hold our infinity
in your heart,
keep me forever.

Take me beyond the
end take me to
paradise, where your
beauty is the
orchid, the heaven.

Hold me in your heart,
hold me in your mind, I want
to live in your
heart as a beat of hope.

SORRY

I am coming today
with empty hands,
I have nothing to hold, just
the truth in my heart, I am sorry
if I say that I love you,
I'm sorry if I can't hold
my feelings anymore, but
I need to tell you
how much I love you,
how much I need you.

MAKING LOVE

What if we make love?

You will caress me with
your beauty, and I will caress
you with poetry.

BLESSING

When I saw you
for the first time, I felt joy
in my soul, and my life
changed dramatically just
because I saw you.
I bless the day
that my eyes saw you; I bless
my eyes for the
opportunity to see you every
single day,
I thank God I have you
by my side.

Please, never leave me; I beg you
to be with me, because I want
to spend the rest of my life
with you.

ROAD

I was lost
before I met you,
my heart had no direction,
and my feet got tired
from long walks,
before I met you,
I was lost.

POET

Let me write in your
radiant gaze my desire
to be a poet, give me
the honor to love you, if I cannot
love you the way you
deserve, please; I beg you
to teach me how, because
I am ready to learn.

SUGAR

Even though you are far
from me, I can feel you; your
love keeps me warm, and
your sugar kisses
quench my thirst.

My heart beats fast, and my desires
become peace; your giant
light covers me with
your fresh feelings.

Now I know what it feels like
to be in love.

TELL ME

I don't even know if
I suffer for loving you or
for forgetting you; I don't know.

If you taught me how
to love you, please, teach me
with your memories how
to forget you,
because my life
isn't exact since you left me.

Open your heart and tell me
the truth, don't worry
if your words make me cry; let
me tell you a little
secret, my heart is crying,
broken, destroyed
because of you, be brave
enough and face
your feelings if you have.

Gerbin Miche

IF YOU COULD SEE ME

If your eyes could see me right now,
you would realize
how much I love you,
if your eyes could read my lips
right now, you would realize
that I can't stop saying
your name, if you could
see me right now, you will realize
that I need you.
I have kept moons in my soul
and a handful of
stars in my hands
to crown you, sweet lady, I have
blank sheets
to write your name and
dark nights to bright me
with your light, I have
in the pocket of my shirt
a red carnation
to lull your heart, I have
in my violin a musical note
to compose
a melody just for you, I have
in my heart a sigh to
kiss you and to kiss you over and over.

IN MY DREAMS

When I close my eyes,
I dream of you, and I swear
that you are my favorite
place to rest, with you I renew
my strength, I find peace
and joy, you are
my faithful romance,
when I am with you,
I have no fear.

When I dream about you,
everything is true;
when I dream, I feel so happy;
you make me happy.

PRETTY GIRL

Beautiful like sunrise,

soft like silk between hands,

tender as a baby's caress,

delicate as rose petal,

fresh like a spring breeze.

God made you with his mighty hands,
his masterpiece.

You are woman, beautiful
and brave, smart and unique.

I WILL LOVE YOU

I will love you because
you are perfect
in your imperfections.

I will love you because
I was born to
love you.

I will love you because
you deserve to be loved.

I will love you with all my strength.

I will always love you, no
matter what happens, in my tribulations
I will love you, in
my happiness I will love you,
in my sadness I will love you, I will
love you forever.

WHAT POETRY IS?

Poetry is when your peace
caresses my heart,
poetry is drinking honey
from your lips,
poetry is drinking the
sweetness of life from your soul.

Poetry is you.

Poetry is your infinite beauty;
poetry is your sincerity,
poetry is your humble heart,
poetry is you and me together.

I WANT TO BE

I want to be your new dawn,
I want you to be my life.

I want to be the air
that plays with your hair, the
oxygen you breathe.

I want to wake up
every day
next to you and look at myself
in your brown eyes.

I would like to be a poet
to write you poetry, I want to be
the sigh of your heart,
I want to be your perfect
shelter on your
cold nights.

I just want to be yours.

YOUR SWEETNESS

You are a sweet poetry
in my life, my perfect retreat,
sunshine of my life,
without you, I don't know
what to do, I need you
to guide my way.

Your sweetness fills me
with love and
makes me a better
person, your sweetness
is the bread I need
to satisfy my hunger.

WAY OF LOVE

You are the infinite path,
the light my soul
seeks, the hope that
makes me live, faith to love.

You are my strong thought; I will
always love you.

I choose to love you
because loving you is a
gift from God.

YOU

Every time you see me,
you kiss my soul, every
time I see you, I feel joy.

There is no special time
or day to show you love,
to respect you, to trust you;
I do it every single second
of my life, with all the
power of my heart because
I fell in love with you,
you only you have the
power to make me
fall in love every day.

My love belongs to you and yours to me.

MASTERPIECE

My eyes
have seen
beautiful days,
new dawns;
I have seen
the sun
hiding behind the
clouds, I have
seen flowers
bloom and
the seeds
germinate; I have
seen beautiful
moments, but
someone like you,
this is my first time.

Holy God! You are God's masterpiece.

AMBER EYES

Today I want to write you
poetry, I don't even know
how, but I want to write.

My heart feels joy
my voice sings your
name, oh darling! Today I want
to call you honey.

Honey—you are the
first flower in my garden,
the first star in my sky,
my first romance,
my first love.

From heaven you are the
sweetest verse of poetry,
the first red carnation
of love, the first song
of King David, you are a real
woman, a real
treasure, your gaze caresses
my soul,
my little woman of
amber eyes.

I WILL CHOOSE YOU

I close my eyes to dream
with you, and I dream with
you to be alive; there is
no shadow in
my imagination, no sadness
on my mind, only
you are on my mind.

I drew you in my dreams, and
you appeared
in my reality.
You saw me
with your two golden eyes
shining like the
sun at noon; you unchained me,
you broke my fears, and
you taught me to be strong; that's
why I will always
choose you, you are
my source of life.

LOSING MY HEAD

I gave you, my kisses
I gave you, my hugs
I gave you everything I had
deep inside, everything;
in exchange, I got pain,
sadness, and loneliness;
I gave you all my rainy and
sunny days; I gave you
the strength of
my blood, the power
of my feelings, I did everything
just to spend the
rest of my life with you,
I gave you my trust,
my warmth, honesty, I gave you
my faith, I gave you
my life; now I understood
that you never loved me, but
no matter what you did
or what you will do to me,
remember, I still love you
the same way I loved you yesterday.

WITHOUT YOU

Today I am full of sadness,
my eyes can't cry; I have
only sweet memories of you,
my pencil writes what
my heart says; I want
nobody near me, I want
no hugs from
anyone else, I want no
kisses from nobody else, I want
only your memories to
calm down my tears; I hear
a bell ringing in the distance
and its sound reminds me
that you are far from me,
I don't know what to do.
I'm sad, and although I don't want
to dream about you anymore,
your love helps me to
stay alive; without you, I am just
a paramo, I no longer smell
your scent in the air, your
voice no longer kisses my senses,
I don't have enough strength
to go on, only my notebook
handles my tears.

I'm sad my eyes can't cry
my heart does, and you

aren't here to listen to me, I will
stop writing poetry, I no longer
have inspiration,
There is silence inside me.

WHEN I SEE YOU

Every time I see you, I feel so happy,
I feel like a new
man,
every time I see you, I discover
the universe.

When I see your smile, I see a new world.

Your smile is a garden
where my dreams come true,
your smile has the
power that I need to stand up.

When I see you smiling, I think I belong
to you, and I swear I kiss
heaven just because
I see you smiling.
I don't want to be far away from you,
so I beg you to hold me tight forever.

HAPPINESS

It is impossible not to love
your sweetness because when
I embrace myself, I smell
your perfume all over
my skin, it is impossible
not to love myself because
I breathe only for you; I am a
piece of land on the
horizon, and with your
warmth, my day begins.

Your sweetness, your kisses restore
me like the sun
restores the cloudy day
to make it shine.
You are my spring poem,
the golden treasure
of my life, the
white rose of my dreams,
that's why I love you, and
I want you to be
with me for the rest of my life.

It is impossible not to love your sweetness,
it is impossible not to love you.

My eyes see through your simplicity,
your clarity; you are the
truth of a new beginning, my true inspiration,
true love.

I SWEAR

I see the light in your heart,
the love that guides my way,
you are the reason for
my life, the water that
quenches my thirst, and
I promise never to stop loving you,
because since I met
you, you have been in my soul.
Now I know that
you are my star and
only you make my night shine.
I swear, my love for you
will never end because
my passion is made from fire and water,
doesn't know fear, and doesn't
have boundaries.

I swear I will always be with you.

IN MY HANDS

I have in my hands
a verse for you: I was
born to love you, and
I live only to love you.
I will give you
my life, the strength of
my blood to love you, to
protect you.

The way I love you, the way I need you.

I need your peace to
calm down my fears because
without you, I am just
a man looking for someone.

FREEDOM

I chained my freedom
to be free.

There is no love
without pain.

There are no roses
without thorns.

There is no sweetness
before drinking bitterness.

There is no forgiveness
without repentance.

There is no miracle
without faith.

There is light,
there is darkness.

You are my light.

I want to love you
the way you love me.

You love me as a sinner,
but you hate my sins.

MYSTERY OF LOVE

Her beauty has mystery,
her eyes magnificence,

her body a touch
of philosophy,

sometimes she turns
into a handful of soil and
a drop of water.

What do I need to do
to read her?

What do I need to do to love her?

Her beauty has mystery.

LITTLE GIRL

When you look at me, you
build my life with your
tenderness, sweet-looking girl.
You are the wind
pushing the caravels
in the sea, in your emerald eyes
the deep sea anchors
its mysteries, happy
my soul that sees your light
sees your exceptional beauty;
you are a ray of sun breaking
the clouds of
the infinite sky, a humble
verse prayer to heaven.
Oh, girl, yes, my little girl! With just
one look from your pure
eyes, you change my life,
your voice has magic, and
you cast a spell on
my heart, little by little I discover
your galaxy, your existence,
finding you, I find out my life,

I realize love.

My sweet little girl.

SHE

I love her the
way I never loved before,
I love her:
beauty,
her face,
her eyes,
her body,
her figure,
her skin,
I love her imperfections,
I love her so much.

I give her my feelings, all
my decisions, I give her my life.

EVERY DAY

Sometimes I wish I had the
courage, the same courage
that I have when alone
in my room I write and pronounce
your name thousands
of times, only your name
can be written
in my notebook, in my heart.
It is true, I just want to
write your name day and night,
and have the courage to
tell you: I am so happy,
thanks to you.
When you are by my side,
everything looks perfect,
being with you
I discovered my strength
and I accepted all
my weaknesses, I have learned
that without you, I am nothing.
It is true; I want to tell you
that I love you, I need you,

I really like to know everything
about you, I want you
to know that the beats
of my heart are for you,
I sigh only for you.

Every day I need you,
every day I need more and more of you.

LOVE

Love is the most beautiful
feeling in life; sometimes
it hurts a lot, love is not
saying only beautiful words
or just giving caresses
and hugs.
Love is feeling the
rain and the sun's warmth
on the skin.
Love is not boastful; love
means respect, friendship,
and forgiveness for ourselves.
Love forgives everything; love
doesn't know hate or resentment,
but it does know tears,
sadness, and joy, love doesn't
argue anything, love is
a philosophy that we
don't understand, love is a
theology that
we should know, love means
to have a humble
heart, sincere, honest, and
free-spirited.

Love is pure and sincere,
love is perfect, love is
a source of living water,
love means life and wisdom.
Love heals all pain we feel,
Love is love.

Love is not a feeling; it is a decision.

SUNRISE AND SUNSET

You turned me into the rain;
you turned me into water.

You turned me into a handful of soil,
you turned me into dust.

You turned me into sun,
you turned me into the moon.

You turned me into a star;
you turned me into glitter.

You made me fire; you made me fathom.

You turned me into wind; into a whirlwind.

I turned into sin, into hell.

You turned me into a troubadour in a soft verse.

You made me a bohemian;
you made me a young man.

You made me strong, you made me great.

I am dawn and dusk.

Today I am: a troubadour, bohemian, fire,
water, light, shadow, storm, stone, infinite,
free and dreamy, sometimes crazy, sometimes winner.

You free me.

YOU LEAVE ME

I gave you everything I had
and what I didn't have; I gave
you the strength of my blood,
I gave you my advice,
I gave you my best moments,
my joys and tears, I gave you
my triumphs and defeats,
I gave you my sunny and cloudy days,
I gave you everything
I owned, I wrote for you beautiful poems,
amazing verses;
I gave you the song of my heart,
the ink of my pen,
the inspiration of my soul,
I gave you everything
without measure,
I gave you all my talent.

Today you leave me; wherever you go,
I wish you the best; remember, you'll always be
my sweet little princess.

God bless you today, tomorrow, and always,
my sweet little princess.

DUST

Sometimes I am scared,

and sometimes I am brave enough.

I am a man full of mystery,

I write happiness and sadness,

sometimes my tears

wash away all my feelings and desires

just to be a new human being.

My verses are everything I have;

I am the perfect creation,

I am perfect in my imperfection,

I am dust and ash.

ELEMENTS

My body is a handful of soil,

and my soul a breath of life.

Sometimes my thoughts burn

their thoughts, and my head

doesn't know why.

My heart seeks water

to quench yesterday's thirst

while tomorrow awaits

today's dream.

MÍA ABRIL

Red lips, stunning body;
your name synonymous with life,
you are an eternal orchid,
your beauty shines
like the sun at noon,
like gold in a king's crown.

You are the melody of
King David, the poetry
of King Solomon.

Abril—sweet little girl,
nothing compares to you,
not even the whole world
with all its glory, nothing.

You will always be my inspiration,
the ink that pours out
sweetness on my book,
your tenderness lights up
my life.

Mía Abril, take my hands
and my whole life too,
I belong to you.

ALL

I offer you in a glass
of wine the madness
of my life; I offer you my roses
and thorns, my dreams,
my whole life.
I offer you everything, even things
that I don't own.
My verses that I am writing today.
The garden of poetry,
the fugitive kiss that
I thought was mine.
I offer you water from my humble
heart to quench
your sunny days.

I offer you my heart, simplicity, and my will,
I present you everything
to be by your side.

FAREWELL

Today I should say goodbye
to you, goodbye, little princess,
my beloved sweetheart.
Will you forget me? I don't know yet.
One thing I'm sure,
you will kiss another
man, and all my kisses
will be erased from your lips.
I promise myself never
to forget you; I will keep
your caresses as the ground
keeps the root
of the tree after being felled.
I will walk away from you to see
you happy because
your happiness is mine too.

I will treasure your memories,
all the sweet kisses and hugs.

I will go away, but not alone,
you will come with me because
I own your memories, because
you are in my soul.

I LOVE YOU

It's downing; it is another
beautiful day to say I love you.

I love you differently, in a new
way that I invented to love you,
honestly; this is the first
time that I love somebody, the other
loves in my life were just
whims of my feelings,
feelings that pushed me
to love someone that I don't love,
fleeting passions,
ephemeral perhaps, but that
doesn't stop them
from being beautiful, important
in my life.
I love you with all
my imperfections, with the strength
of my few virtues; that's
how I love you.
I love you in a way
that I don't even understand,
I love you with the
power that sometimes makes me weak,

I love you in an incomparable,
incomprehensible way,
but I love you.
I love you, and I was born to love you
because I already loved you before
I met you.
I thank God for giving me
the honor to meet you; I thank your
parents for letting you be born,
and I thank you for taking care
of yourself to be next to me.

LOVE, LOVE, LOVE

Cuddle me, and don't say
anything; just cuddle me.

I will love you for the
rest of my life, as the flowers
love their beauty and perfume,
like a river loves its stream.
I will love you, like
heaven loves me, and I will
take care of you as
the lion takes care
of his cub, I will be by your
side to support you
and I will never let you down.

I love you with the
piece of heaven, with the strength
of the earth, I love you
with the mighty wind
and the sea; I love you with
warmth of a sunny day and the
mystery night.

I love you—thousands of times
in different ways.

BREEZE

Like a soft spring breeze,
you took over my senses;
you took over my life.

Your shining eyes
are permanent light
that brightens my path.

Your kisses are fresh spring
water, your beauty
illuminates the whole world,
and your voice awakens
my feelings and I touch
the firmament.

Your honey skin caresses
my heart and body,
like a soft spring breeze
you took over my senses.

YOU

You are the orchid
that brightens my days,
your gaze captivates
my soul, and your voice
strolls like blackbirds
on my balcony every morning.

Your beauty is a sacred fragrance
in my life.

You are the girl
who breaks my stony heart;
you are the ink
of my pen; you are everything
I want.

SINCE YOU LEFT ME

Oh, sweetheart! Since you left me, the sun
doesn't light up my window,
the rain has forgotten about my garden;
the wind has been
silent.

Since you left me,
the sea has drowned
in its tears of salty
loneliness; spring doesn't
want to bloom,
since you left me, the hummingbird
no longer drinks honey
from flowers.

Since you are not here,
oblivion is eternal,
and my poetry has forgotten
about me.

SWEETNESS

From vineyards, I have drank
the sweetest wines; from gardens,
I have cut holy flowers;
from banquets, I have been eating
the best dishes.

My eyes have contemplated
bare pores, my hands
have stolen lingerie;
and my lips have kissed
genuine jewels.

I have drank fresh
water from water sources;
from nights, I have
taken forbidden pleasures.
I haven't denied any
pleasure to my body,
even so, I'm thirsty for your passion.

GIRL

You were never
the girl of my dreams,
but since I met you,
you have become
the girl of my life.

A BETTER PLACE

There is nothing sweeter
than being in love
with you; there is
no better place than
living in your heart;
there is nothing
more precious and
romantic than hearing
your lips pronouncing
my name.

A MORTAL MAN

Today fire runs through
my veins; my heart has
a river of poetry.

My soul trembles while
pronouncing your name,
and my blood runs from
head to toe.

Look at me; I get nervous
when you are next to me.

Your beauty is a poem that
conquers my being with
its glory and takes me beyond
infinity; your voice
makes my skin bristle; I am
just a mortal man
in front of you.

I love you, and I like you; I am
so pleased to know
that I love you. During the day
I think of you, dreaming of
being in your arms, your warmth
caresses my skin, and when
the night falls, I kiss you

until you are breathless.
Our love is a poem written
on fire, written on water, and
no one can break it.

When I think of you,
I feel peace, so I write and
pronounce your name.
It is enough for me to know
that I am the man who loves you, and
you are the woman who
makes me happy.

KNOWLEDGE

I am a master of my beliefs
and a student of my mistakes.
I'm sweetness of my triumphs,
brave of my defeats; I'm a
verse of loneliness, my life
is drop of water in the
passing storm.
My knowledge is knowing
that I exist and I'm worth
more than worldly glory;
my actions
are my destiny. I have
learned that my weakness
makes me stronger
because I always believe
in myself.
I climb mountains of
adversity because I'm sure
life today is accurate; if I have
no dreams, tomorrow doesn't
exist, and yesterday is
only past because today is today,
and here I am to be happy.
Today I tell you: life is a battlefield;
our destiny is to fight
until the end; make life
your master, and you will gain

knowledge, but if you
listen to foolish advice,
you will reap thorns.
Listen to your heart and act
wisely, your will is the
strength of your life, and your efforts
will be the glory of your achievements.
Smile, cry, and be happy, the greatest
virtue is knowing that God loves us
and his mercy doesn't disappoint us.
Fight with courage, and be brave because
life is not easy, but not impossible to
make dreams come true.

LIFE WILL PASS

I will remember you every
single day of my life, and you,
you will fall from the tree
like a dry leaf; you will
forget about me when you
sleep with another man.
Yesterday you were mine,
and today you belong
to him; perhaps tomorrow
you will forget about yesterday.
Tomorrow you'll erase all
memories from mind, maybe
you loved me as I loved you too, or
perhaps I yet love you; I don't know.
One thing I'm sure,
your memories will come
with me because of a pact
between you and me.
Today I write you these
verses; if one day you read them,
I beg you to forgive me
for not putting out the fire
of your vile deceit.
I never dreamed of disappointment;
I drank bitterness from
your heart; I dreamed of living
together; my faith remained a stream

to the silence of oblivion.
If tomorrow by coincidence we see each other on
the street if my lips and gaze don't smile
at you, you will know that I have
forgotten you.
A song, a memory, an instant; I don't know, I will
continue to remember you without
pronouncing your name because you were mine.
Tomorrow the rose bushes will bloom;
perhaps you will say my name.
today as tomorrow, the hours, days, and years
will pass, a new spring will come, and life
will go on, like wind in autumn, time will remove
memories of you from my mind, then I will
say that I don't know you, I never met you.

LIFE

Life has secrets of sweetness,
drowsiness, and a bit
of bitterness.

Life is a fertile land
where everything we sow
we reap, it is a page
where we write our story.
Life is like rain, rhythmic and blessed;
it falls on the earth, and
the grass becomes green.

Life is beautiful, sometimes easy,
sometimes challenging,
but never impossible to make
dreams come true.
Life makes us cry, occasionally sad,
sometimes happy.
Life is a treasure, it is a gift
from God, life finds no joy
in the pleasure of the flesh; it doesn't
rejoice in vanity; life
is dignity, respect, self and mutual love.

THIRSTY

Allow me to drink from
your lips your sweetness,

from your body
the pleasure,

invite me to have
a bite of the forbidden
fruit,

and drink from your pores
your naked desires.

I want you to be mine, just as I'm yours.

FLOWER

Love is like a flower,
if you water it a lot, it might
get disease; if you don't,
it will wither.

Love is like a flower; if today
you don't appreciate its
beauty, tomorrow, you will
regret its existence.

ETERNAL FLOWER

Like fresh spring water,
pure and clean, beautiful
as a flower in the garden
of heaven, sweet
and tender, magical,
dreamy angel; that's how you are.

Lauren, not even the heavens
nor the earth compares to you,
to your beauty.
Your beauty has mysteries
and tenderness that go far beyond
infinite; your beauty means life;
your sparkling brown eyes
are stars in the sky and have
the sweetness of ripe grapes, your
unwavering gaze is a sizzling summer,
tender spring, magical, that
makes the whole world
fall in love with you.
Your voice has great sweetness,
is the song of a nightingale, and makes
the ends of the earth beat, the waters
of the rivers, seas, and lakes
in your humble heart sings.
Oh, Kerr! You are a mystical rose
in a garden of love, you are

classic poetry of King Solomon;
you are an enchanted paradise
whispering glories, your soul is
humble and fertile, is the soil
where the wheat seeds germinate; you are light
and hope for a glorious day, your
simplicity is a ray of sunshine that caresses
the flowers of the countryside.
You are unique like the sun and moon,
like the heavens and earth, you are
a perfect creation, the daughter of
a perfect God.

I bless the day I met you, I bless God
for giving me the honor of meeting you.

SPRING FLOWER

From your soul, I will steal
your beauty to write you
poetry.
Today, let me be your
poet, and you be my muse.

Larson, there is no better
poem than the splendor
of your beauty, nor is there
a beautiful rose than
the nature of your blessed existence;
birds and flowers rejoice
while contemplating
your magnificence; your essence
is a brave kiss of consecration
that goes up to heaven.

Your eyes are two stars
in the galaxy, your blue eyes
are deep oceans, and in their immensity,
the waters rejoice.

My heart gets inspiration
from your poetic soul, from
your garden of love.

Oh, Larson! Your heart

is a bouquet in the garden
of Eden; your docile soul
has the strength of obedience
and the peace of simplicity.

Your sweetness is a romance of love
you are eternal spring flower,
flower of joy, brave woman.

www.ingramcontent.com/pod-product-compliance
Lightning Source LLC
Chambersburg PA
CBHW020335130626
46549CB00003B/1180